ISS…
to…

S…
O…

Editor: **Cara Acred**

ISSUE 66

Independ… …blishers

First published by Independence
The Studio, High Green, Great Shelford
Cambridge CB22 5EG
England

British Library Cataloguing in Publication Data

Sexual orientation – (Issues today; v. 66)

1. Sexual orientation – Juvenile literature . 2. Gender identity – Juvenile literature.
3. Sexual minorities – Juvenile literature.

I. Series II. Acred, Cara.

306.7'6-dc23

ISBN-13: 9781 86168 630 5

Acknowledgements

The publisher is grateful for permission to reproduce the following material.

While every care has been taken to trace and acknowledge copyright, the publisher tenders its apology for any accidental infringement or where copyright has proved untraceable. The publisher would be pleased to come to a suitable arrangement in any such case with the rightful owner.

Chapter One: Being LGB or T

Am I gay? Are you born gay? Can you stop being gay?, © AVERT, 2011, *Parents' stories*, © FFLAG 2010, *Being LGB or T at school*, © 2008 - 2012 CSIE, *The business case for diversity*, © Opportunity Now 2012, *Trans terminology*, © Channel 4/ Flamingo, *LGB & T timeline'*, © NHS North West, *'My trans daughter'*, © Department of Health 2011.

Chapter Two: LGBT Rights

My homophobic bullying story, © Department of Health 2011, *Homophobic crime*, © Crown copyright, *More gay couples tie the knot*, © Telegraph Media Group Limited 2012, *Social exclusion and sexual orientation*, © 2012 Stonewall, *Factbox: lesbian, gay, bisexual and transgender rights around the world*, © 2012 Thomson Reuters Foundation.

Illustration on page 21 is by Angelo Madrid. All other illustrations, including the cover, are by Don Hatcher.

Editorial by Christina Hughes and layout by Jackie Staines, on behalf of Independence Educational Publishers.

Printed in Great Britain by MWL Print Group Ltd.

Cara Acred
Cambridge
September 2012

Am I gay? Are you born gay? Can you stop being gay?

Information from AVERT.

Am I gay?

Many people feel attracted to people of the same sex, and wonder if this means that they are gay. For some people these feelings can be very intense and alienating. Some people who ask themselves the question 'am I gay?' are indeed gay, and go on to have gay sexual relationships. But other people find that these feelings change over time.

Some people are bisexual, meaning they are attracted to both men and women, and have relationships with both. Some people are not attracted to anyone and wonder if this is a sign that they are gay. Often it is only time that will resolve these questions.

When do people know that they are gay?

There is no simple answer to this question, as it varies from person to person. Deciding you are gay often happens gradually and it can feel very confusing.

During research carried out with young gay men in the UK, the men interviewed described a set of feelings which they gradually realised made them 'different' in some way, feelings they thought maybe every teenage boy has.

'I thought, well, this is just the phase bit. Sooner or later I'm going to start finding women attractive. I never did. As I became more attracted to men, and I still wasn't getting attracted to women, I thought, s**t, you're gay. And it was really quite a shock when it hit me.' Luke

With time, someone who is gay will realise that they are sexually attracted to members of the same sex, and that it is not 'a phase'. This realisation could come at any time during their lives. Many people become aware of gay feelings during their teenage years, as this is when they begin to learn more about their sexuality and identity. However, many gay people don't identify themselves as gay until much later on in life.

'After college I spent nearly 15 years trying to deny to myself who I was... a gay man. Finally, at age 38, I began to accept the fact that I was gay.'

Is being gay a phase young people go through?

For some people yes, and for others, no.

Some people do not have their first homosexual feelings or experience until they are adults.

There is evidence that for some people homosexual experiences are part of an experimental phase when they are younger. This kind of behaviour is perfectly normal.

Am I gay? Are you born gay? Can you stop being gay?

Are you born gay? What causes people to be gay?

There is no simple answer to the question, 'Are some people born lesbian or gay?' Some scientists think that we are born with our sexuality already determined.

'How can science tell you what I am? I mean I've had boyfriends, and was happy with them, had girlfriends and may have boyfriends again for all I know. If it's a gay gene what's going on? Is it just turning itself on and off in my head? It doesn't feel like biology, it feels like love.'
Jo

Others believe that a combination of emotional and social factors can determine sexuality. People's behaviour is influenced by their family environment and their experiences. Beliefs about sex are at first shaped by family values. Later on these beliefs may be shaped by pleasant and unpleasant experiences of sex and also shape their choice of activities and partners. Throughout their life a person's sense of who and what they are has a strong impact on their sexual development and experience.

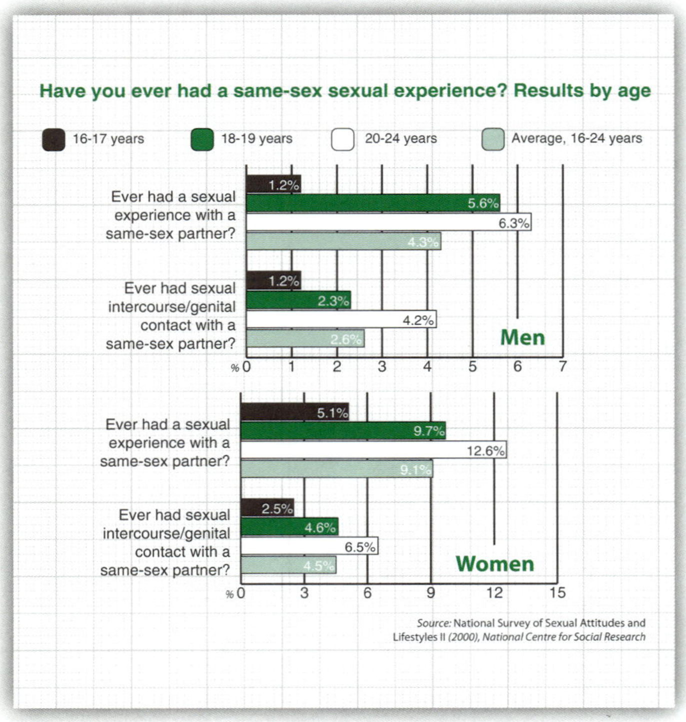

Can you stop being gay?

Many people are interested in whether sexuality can be changed if a person desires to. Organisations that help homosexuals attempt to change their sexuality can be generally divided between those that use psychological methods and those that use religious 'healing' methods.

Some people believe homosexuality is an illness and believe it can and should be cured.

The American Psychological Association (APA), the world's largest association of psychologists, has stated that:

'Homosexuality is not a mental disorder and the APA opposes all portrayals of lesbian, gay and bisexual people as mentally ill and in need of treatment due to their sexual orientation.'

Some strongly religious groups believe that homosexuality is sinful and goes against the Bible and other religious texts. There is little to no science behind the healing techniques used.

Gay and lesbian rights organisations argue that these views misunderstand what it means to be gay, and amount to discrimination against gay and lesbian people. Furthermore, the APA has carried out a review, which concludes that psychological interventions are not successful at changing sexual orientation and that they can cause significant harm.

Mini glossary

Bisexual *– a person who is attracted to both men and women*

Discrimination *– unfair treatment against someone because of the group/class they belong to*

Experimental [phase] *– exploring both emotional and sexual feelings by trying and experiencing new things*

Homosexual *– a person who is attracted to members of the same sex as themselves*

Information from AVERT. © AVERT, 2011

www.avert.org

Parents' stories

The families of gay and lesbian young people share their experiences of learning about their relative's sexual orientation.

Janet J's story

The day started out normally enough. Glyn, 19, was home from university for the weekend. He was due to leave on the Sunday afternoon, so we went out for an early pub lunch. My husband and I both had our mouths full of roast beef when, in a quiet voice, Glyn broke the silence with 'I've got something to tell you – I'm gay'. Now, some parents say they already had their suspicions, but not us, not an inkling. The thoughts rushed through my head: what had we done to cause this, had I mothered him too much? Was this a passing phase? Glyn assured us that he'd known since his early teens that he was gay, and that he was sure it was just the way he was born. After all, his older brother was brought up in the same way and he was straight. Then the worries set in: surely he'd be dead with AIDS before the year was out; if not that, then he'd get beaten up every time he went out. He'd always be sad and lonely, and would be discriminated against in every aspect of life.

Glyn had obviously thought about our likely reactions and tried to allay our fears, but as soon as we'd left him at the station, the tears flowed. It felt a bit like bereavement, a grieving for the life I had planned for him: the happy and successful life, the daughter-in-law, the grandchildren. When we got home, my husband (much calmer than me!) suggested we sit down and write a list of 'what could be worse'. That soon put things into perspective. We thought of other young people we knew who were suffering from mental or life-threatening illnesses, or who were into a life of alcohol, drug abuse or crime – and just being gay suddenly didn't look so bad.

Like many women, I needed to talk – a lot! I was fortunate to have friends I could turn to but, best of all, I found FFLAG – Families and Friends of Lesbians and Gay Men. It was wonderful to talk to someone who knew just how I felt. Once I'd come to terms with Glyn's sexuality, I decided to help establish the first helpline and support group in Wales, and it's been wonderful to have been able to help so many other mums and dads over the years to realise that their child's sexuality is only a small part of their life, and that they are still the same dearly-loved child they always were. We say that being gay is just like being left-handed – a bit unusual, a bit inconvenient at times, but in general not a major problem. And Glyn – he's been with his lovely partner for nine years now, they've bought a house together, he has a successful career and lots of friends. It's all good now!

> **"We thought of other young people we knew who were suffering from mental or life-threatening illnesses, or who were into a life of alcohol, drug abuse or crime – and just being gay suddenly didn't look so bad."**

Parents' stories

A sister's story

My 'little sister' came out over 14 years ago. She was married, although separated from her husband, and had a young son. It simply never occurred to me that she was anything other than heterosexual. The only thing that upset me on hearing her news, was that I felt that somehow I should have known. I felt guilty that I had not been more supportive and I really worried that she had been very unhappy over the years.

Our parents' reaction was initially hostile and very negative. I was living hundreds of miles away at the time, and know that my sister had a very difficult time of it. Our father would put the phone down if my sister's partner happened to answer it. Our mother often became quite hysterical and tearful. Gradually things changed and they adjusted to the fact that one of their daughters happened to be a lesbian. And over the years they came to love my sister's partner as a true member of the family too.

What saddens me is that various pressures mean that neither my sister nor her partner is 'out' at work. My sister works for a multi-national company and says that if her work colleagues found out that she was gay she would lose respect and her authority. For me, my little sister's sexuality is not an issue. It's not something I think about. However, I know that life is still not as easy as it should be for my sister and her partner. The other day we were discussing the fact that they need a new bed. Bed manufacturers recommend that you and your partner test the suitability of the mattress by lying on it in the shop. I said that I thought this was a good idea – and she looked doubtfully at me. 'What do you think they would say in the shop if Liz and I lay down on the bed together?' It simply hadn't occurred to me that anyone would take issue or that my sister and her partner would be uncomfortable doing that. I have a lot to learn!

'As part of the school curriculum on relationships and sex education, children should be taught that gay relationships are exactly equal in status to heterosexual relationships.'

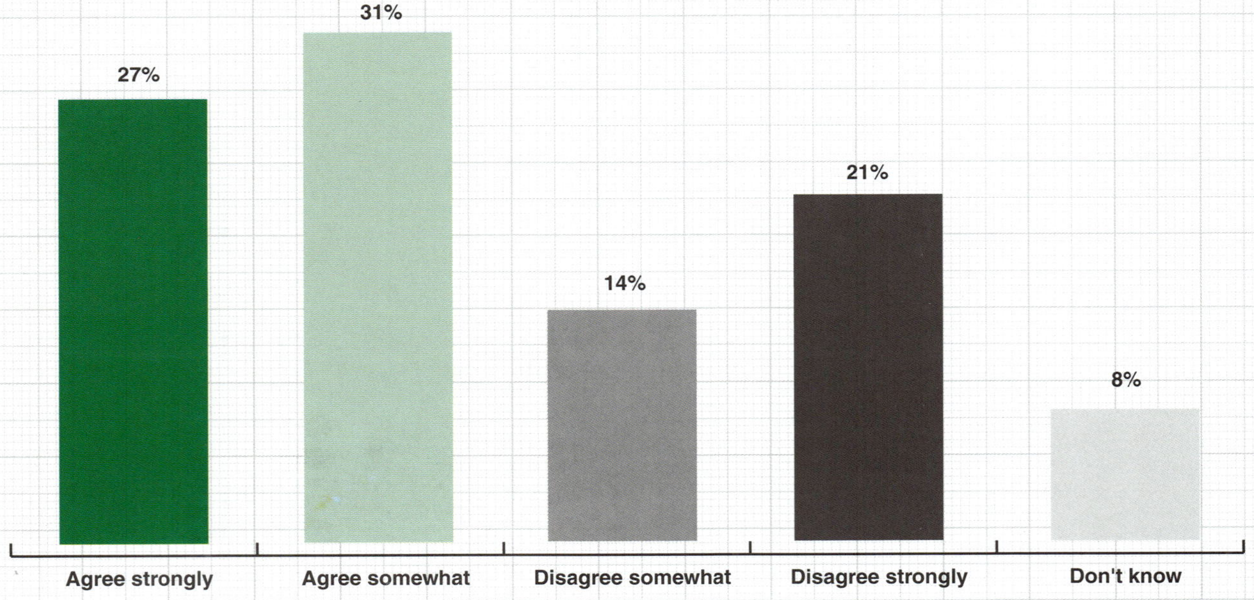

Fieldwork: 9-11 March 2012 Base: 1,000.
Source: Gay Britain Survey. Prepared on behalf of The Times by Populus. © Populus

Parents' stories

Bruce's story

For most of my adult life I have been involved in charismatic Christian churches and was a pastor for many years. We brought our five children up to follow the Scriptures and it never occurred to us that one might be gay. One day, however, I felt a strong inner conviction that one of my sons was gay. This caused great inner turmoil and I didn't say anything about it to anyone for a long time but it led me to begin to quietly research what homosexuality is and what the Bible actually teaches about it.

My understanding at the time had been that homosexuality was a perversion brought about by wrong family relationships like a remote, uncaring father figure and an oppressive, dominant mother figure. Although this didn't really describe our family, I knew there had been too many times when I had been off 'looking after the flock' rather than with my family. So I was going through a personal hell, battling a sense of guilt as well as shame. Next I went through a period of mourning. I would like to say this was an unselfish mourning for our son and the difficulties he was going through but the truth is it was mostly selfish. How was I going to tell my wife, family and friends? What would the church think and what would become of my ministry?

It seemed to me that there were three fundamental barriers to understanding the truth.

1. The thought that surely the Church can't all be wrong on this issue.
2. The conviction that it is unnatural to have same-sex attraction.
3. Anyway, the Bible clearly condemns it.

Number 1 barrier was easy. The 'Church' has rarely all agreed on anything. In fact, the 'Church' has regularly got it badly wrong – from the days of the Apostles when they thought slavery was OK, even to today when most denominations still don't treat women as equals to men.

Number 2 barrier was easily enough to hurdle intellectually but more difficult emotionally. It didn't take much study to discover that homosexuality occurs naturally throughout the animal kingdom. For some people, attraction to the opposite sex is natural for them. The difficult part was that, for me, homosexual sex seemed disturbingly unpleasant. But then I remembered when my older sister had told me about the 'birds and the bees' when I was quite young and how revolted I had felt about what she had described at the time.

Number 3 barrier came as a bombshell when I understood that so many of us charismatics had been essentially interpreting the Scriptures wrongly, and the way we understood it to teach against homosexuality was just symptomatic.

The Bible is written to point us towards faith in Jesus. There are a lot of things taught in the Bible that we know would be wrong for us to adopt today, such as worshiping more than one god, owning slaves, the death penalty for breaking religious laws, oppressing women, ethnic cleansing and genocide as well as persecution of gays. We need to interpret the Old and the New Testaments in the light of God's law of love. Actually, the Biblical writers had no concept of a loving, faithful, stable gay relationship between two men or two women and so they never addressed the matter.

When my son did eventually come to me to tell me he was gay, by God's grace I had come through most of my negative emotions and was able to hug him and tell him that I loved him and that I was fully supportive of him. It wasn't plain sailing after that though. I told his Mum first and she cried for a long time. His brothers and sisters had serious problems with it and to some degree still do, although we all try to be loving towards each other.

I resigned from pastoring the AOG church so that I could speak freely about this and other issues. My website www.love-amazing.com is my way of standing up for the truth as I understand it. My wife and I joined FFLAG and it is a real joy to be able to help, even in a small way, parents who are going through the same traumas that we went through. Being a part of FFLAG has been enormously encouraging to us because we have met so many caring people who have wisdom and compassion that has been born out of pain.

Mini glossary

Sexual orientation *– a person's sexual identity; defining a person's attraction towards either members of the same sex (homosexual), the opposite sex (heterosexual) or both (bisexual)*

Information from Families and Friends of Lesbians and Gay Men (FFLAG).

www.fflag.org.uk

Being LGB or T at school

Information from Centre for Studies on Inclusive Education (CSIE).

Frequently asked questions on schooling for lesbian, gay, bisexual and transgender children and young people.

Which children are lesbian, gay, bisexual or transgender (LGBT)?

The short answer is that you cannot tell from looking at someone whether or not they are lesbian, gay, bisexual or transgender (LGBT). LGBT people come from all walks of life, are black, brown, white and all shades in between, may or may not be disabled. Some children may look or dress differently to their peers but this does not mean that they identify as LGBT, or that they will when they are older. Some children may not have thought about their sexual or gender identities yet, while others may be unsure. For some, their sexual or gender identity may change over time. Children who have LGBT parents/carers are no more, and no less, likely than children with heterosexual or gender-normative parents/carers to be LGBT themselves. It is also important to recognise that the terms lesbian, gay, bisexual and transgender are not adopted by everyone. For example, some people may prefer to call themselves queer, neutrois or pansexual.

What is meant by 'transgender'?

The term 'transgender', sometimes shortened to 'trans', is a term for people whose gender identity is different from their birth sex.

- Some trans people feel that they are definitely male or female.
- Some people may adopt the term transsexual.
- Others feel that their identities cannot be defined as male or female, and may use a variety of terms to describe themselves, including un-gendered, genderqueer, gender bent, queer or simply human.
- People who cross-dress or identify as transvestite might also describe themselves as transgender.
- Some intersex people may go on to change to the gender with which they identify in later life if they feel that they were assigned to the wrong gender as a baby.

At your school, have you ever been taught about same-sex relationships or lesbian, gay and bisexual (LGB) people?

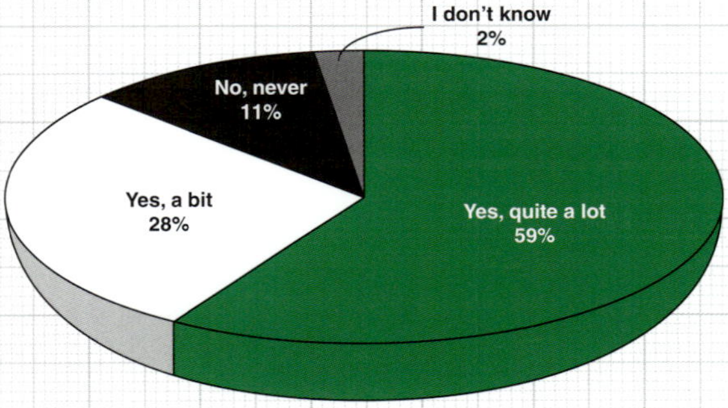

How were you taught about same-sex relationships or lesbian, gay and bisexual (LGB) people?

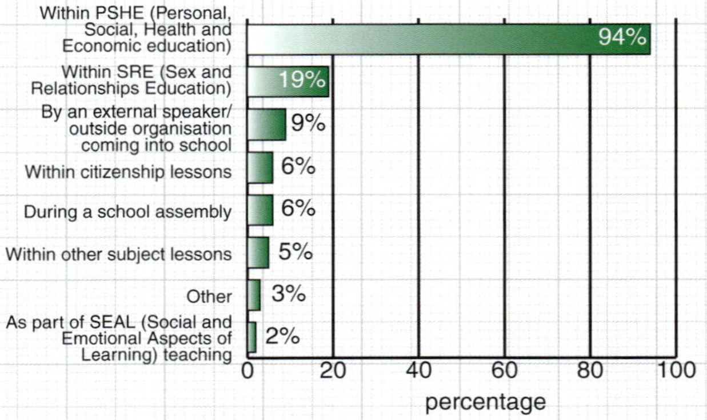

Source: Tackling homophobia and transphobia in settings supporting young people: What are the barriers and facilitators? Findings from a South Yorkshire study. © Sheffield Hallam University, 2011

Being LGB or T at school

We don't have any LGBT people in our school so why do we need to know about them?

- In 2004 it was estimated that there were 124,672 same-gender-attracted pupils in British secondary schools. This is approximately 100 pupils in a school of 2,000.
- Gender variance may be detected in children as young as two, and a high proportion of people who have gender reassignment as adults say that they knew that they were trans while in primary school, even if they lacked the language to express this.
- It is estimated that one in ten adults identify as lesbian, gay or bisexual.
- The number of transgender people within the UK is relatively small but the figures are growing as more people feel able to be open about who they are.

LGBT people – both children and adults – may be less visible within a school than their heterosexual peers. This may be because it feels unsafe for them to be open about who they are, but does not mean that they do not exist. In addition to members of a school community who identify as LGBT themselves, there will also be those who have LGBT members in their immediate or extended family and/or friends.

An important part of schooling is to prepare children and young people for life in the wider world. LGBT people make up a significant part of our society and schools are failing their pupils if they do not educate them about the important role LGBT people have always played, and will continue to play, in the shaping of our society.

CSIE believes that everyone is of equal value, earned by virtue of being human. We believe that diversity is part of what makes the world beautiful; it should be celebrated and used as a rich learning resource. Everyone should be valued and made to feel welcome.

We think that it is inappropriate to talk to very young children about sex so how can we possibly deal with LGBT issues in the classroom?

The age at which teachers speak to children about sex is a matter for individual schools to discuss with parent and governor groups. However, children talk about sex from an early age within the playground and many references to sex exist within popular culture. Schools therefore often feel that it is advisable to educate their pupils. This can and should be done in an age-appropriate manner.

It is unlikely that any school will be teaching very young children about the mechanics of having sex: rather, it is more likely that schools wish to encourage pupils to adopt values about the importance of respect and the promotion of healthy relationships.

Lesbian, gay and bisexual relationships can and should be raised alongside the teaching of heterosexual relationships and gendered identities.

It is important that children from LGBT families feel that their families are recognised, accepted and respected. It is entirely appropriate that discussions amongst very young children revolve around the many different kinds of families that exist within our society. This is one very simple way in which schools can speak about LGBT identities without talking about sex.

Being LGB or T at school

How should schools respond to the multiple uses of the word 'gay'?

Any use of the term 'gay' to mean that something is nonsense, broken or negative should not be tolerated amongst pupils or staff.

Pupils and staff should be encouraged to find alternative expressions that do not criticize a particular sexual identity. A lot of people would not dream of uttering a religious or racial slur. Being lesbian, gay or bisexual is often viewed negatively. Failing to challenge the use of this phrase in this manner supports this view. Schools should think about how to respond to such comments and make sure that all members of staff are committed to stopping it being used in a negative context. At the same time, schools need to make sure that pupils feel they can talk openly about gay identities without fear of being labelled homophobic.

> **We believe that diversity is part of what makes the world beautiful; it should be celebrated and used as a rich learning resource. Everyone should be valued and made to feel welcome.**

What should teachers do if a pupil comes out to us as being LGBT?

Young people come out to staff for a variety of reasons. These may include, but are not limited to, a need for support and information or to change how they are being treated. Young people have told us that they find it helpful when staff thank them for sharing this information with them. For some young people this may be the first time that they have ever talked about their LGBT identity and the process may be nerve-wracking. Young people have also said that they find it helpful when staff listen to them and ask them why they have shared this information.

Why do so many LGBT pupils get bullied?

This group of children and young people face a very real level of violence and hatred within primary and secondary schools. However, it is by no means inevitable that they will be bullied. When LGBT pupils are bullied this is often due to the wider culture of the school, either turning a blind eye, or failing to challenge ways of thinking. It is the duty of all members of staff to ensure that every child is valued and respected within school. Inclusive schools enable young people to be happy, no matter who they are attracted to or what they look like. Where schools encourage safe, welcoming and respectful atmospheres, and where diversity is genuinely valued, homophobia and transphobia are significantly reduced, if not eliminated entirely.

4 February 2011

Mini glossary

Gender-normative – *a person who follows the gender-based expectations of society*

Pink Pound – *referring to the money spent by someone who is gay or lesbian (the purchasing power of the gay community) in Britain*

Neutrois – *some people see this as a third gender – neither male or female (non-gendered class)*

Pansexual – *a person who is attracted to all gender identities*

Gender reassignment – *changing a person's physical appearance to become the opposite sex. This includes altering their external gender organs and hormonal balances*

Homophobia – *the fear or hatred of people who are attracted to the same sex as themselves (e.g. disliking lesbians, gay men and bisexuals)*

Transphobia – *the fear or hatred of people who are transgender or transsexual*

Information from the Centre for Studies on Inclusive Education (CSIE).

www.csie.org.uk/inclusion/faqlgbt.shtml

The business case for diversity

Lesbians, gay men and bisexuals are an important part of the talent pool…

Lesbians, gay men and bisexuals comprise around 6% of the population, or 3.5 million people, according to government estimates.

36% of gay employees will change careers if discrimination is continued.

A third of gay staff hide their sexual orientation from their employers and co-workers, yet 'out' employees in safe environments earn 50% more than their closeted peers.

At least 55% of gay employees facing discrimination report a direct negative work impact.

Approximately 20% of gay employees facing discrimination at work will consider suicide.

… and an important market

74% of gay and 42% of straight consumers are less likely to buy products from companies that hold negative views of lesbians and gay men.

The 'pink pound' is estimated to be worth £70 billion.

Information from Business in the Community. © Opportunity Now 2012

www.bitcdiversity.org.uk

LGB & T timeline

1100 BC – 146 BC
Ancient Greece. Sexual relationships between men are common but there is no explicit homosexual identity.

1787
In Britain, from medieval times onwards, homosexuality is linked to disease. In 1787 a pamphlet warns of 'emasculated foreign singers' whose degeneracy and effeminacy are 'contagious like the pestilence'.

1861
The death penalty for buggery is abolished in England and Wales (abolished in Scotland 1889).

European r
development
resulting fro
theories concl

By contrast, th
moral deprav
happen to any
Castration a

1905
Sigmund Freud, Austrian founder of psychoanalysis, publishes *Three Essays on the Theory of Sexuality* theorising that homosexuality is not a type of madness or disease, but the result of arrested development at a young age. Freud argues that homosexuals should not be punished and homosexuality should not be illegal.

1951
Medical 'cures' for homosexuality (often offered to men convicted of sexual offences instead of a jail sentence) include electric shock treatment, hallucinogenic drugs, aversion therapy and brainwashing techniques. The last such lobotomy is carried out in 1951.

1965
A UK opinion poll finds that 93% of respondents see homosexuality as a form of illness requiring medical treatment.

1967
The Sexual Offences Act legalises private consensual homosexual sex over the age of 21.

1969
The Stonewall Riots – trans and gender non-conforming people are among those at the forefront resisting arrest during a bar raid at the Stonewall Inn, New York. This event marks the start of the LGBT movement.

After po
from the
Task Forc
Psychiat
changes
of homos
disease t

2007
The Equality Act (Sexual Orientation) Regulations outlaw discrimination in the provision of goods, facilities, services, education and public functions on the grounds of sexual orientation.

2010
The Equality Act makes sexual orientation and gender reassignment protected characteristics.

2011
Measures in the proposed Freedom Bill will make it possible for those with historical convictions for consensual gay sex to apply for their record to be deleted from the police national computer.

The above information is from a History Timeline, documenting the challenges and succes
Inclusion and Human Rights Team at NHS North West. © NHS North West.

LGB & T timeline

Mid 19th C
The medical profession
›egins to break down non-
›rocreative sex into different
›erversions' and 'deviations'.
Homosexuality gradually
emerges as a separate
category, and so too the
›mosexual as an individual.

1885
Male homosexual acts are made illegal in Britain through Section 11 of the Criminal Law Amendment Act, known as the Labouchère Amendment.

1869
Hungarian-Austrian doctor Karl-Maria Kertbeny coins the term 'homosexual' which begins to be used more widely in the 1890s.

1897
British sexologist Havelock Ellis publishes *Sexual Inversion*, the first volume in an intended series called *Studies in the Psychology of Sex*. He argues that homosexuality is not a disease but a natural anomaly occurring throughout human and animal history, and should be accepted, not treated. The book is banned in England for being obscene; the subsequent volumes in the series are published in the US and not sold in England until 1936.

Late 19th C – Early 20th C
e largely sees homosexuality as degeneration in individual
sexuality could be the result of the parents' defective genes,
›xample, hysteria, alcoholism, epilepsy or debauchery. Such
t these 'born criminals' should not be locked up in prison but
treated in asylums.
›h medical profession places more emphasis on madness than
›ickedness, perhaps since madness is something that could
l is the only explanation that doesn't undermine social norms.
›nosis used as 'cures' for homosexuality across Europe and
America.

ressure
›al Gay
American
›ociation
›agnosis
y from a
›ndition'.

1981
First cases of what will come to be called AIDS recorded, first referred to as Gay-Related Immune Deficiency (GRID) and even 'gay cancer'. The discovery that other groups are also susceptible, including haemophiliacs, recipients of blood transfusions and intravenous drug users, prompts the coining of a new name, Acquired Immune Deficiency Syndrome (AIDS).

1983
The National Blood Service (then the Blood Transfusion Service) ban men who have sex with men from donating blood. The National Blood Service denies it is homophobic. Campaigns to reform this policy are ongoing.

1992
The World Health Organisation's International Classification of Diseases finally removes the term homosexuality from its list of mental disorders.

1993
Government removes homosexuality from its list of psychiatric disorders in England and Wales (Scottish government removes it in 2000).

2000
Age of consent for homosexual sex equalised with heterosexual sex, set at 16 for the UK and 17 for Northern Ireland.

2002
Adoption and Children Act changed to allow same-sex couples (and all single people regardless of sexual orientation) to adopt.

›&T people in medicine and healthcare through the ages. It was produced by the Equality,
ete Timeline can be seen at http://www.help.northwest.nhs.uk/lgbt_timeline/

'My trans daughter'

Information from Department of Health.

Sharon has a teenage daughter who is transgender. She describes how Nicki was born in a male body but felt from a very young age that she should have been a girl.

'When my child Nick was about two, I realised that he wasn't playing with toys that I expected a boy to play with. He was interested in dolls and girly dressing-up clothes. At that age, it doesn't really matter. You just think they're trying lots of different things, so I never made a fuss about it.

'But when he was four years old, Nick told me that God had made a mistake, and he should have been a girl.

'I asked my GP what I should do. He told me to wait and see, and that it might just be a phase and go away. But it didn't. It got stronger.

'One day when Nick was six, we were in the car, and he asked me when he could have the operation to cut off his "willy" and give him a "fanny". His older cousin had told him about these things.

'I spoke to a friend who's a psychiatrist. He said I should contact the Tavistock Clinic [now The Tavistock and Portman service for children and young people with gender identity issues].

'He also told me that the medical term is "gender dysphoria". When I looked it up online, I found Mermaids, a charity that helps children with gender identity issues and their families.

'I also spoke to my GP again, who referred us to the local mental health unit. The person at the unit had worked at the Tavistock and knew about gender identity issues.

'He was brilliant. It was such a relief to talk to somebody who understood what was going on. I'd blamed myself, but he reassured me that it wasn't my fault. We were then referred to the Tavistock Clinic.

'The team from the Tavistock came to Nick's school and talked to the teachers. They helped the teachers to understand that Nick wasn't being difficult, and that this may or may not be a phase. When a child is this young, you just don't know.'

From Nick to Nicki

'Nicki desperately wanted to be female all the time. When she was ten, we feminised her name from Nick to Nicki at home. The following year, Nicki started secondary school as a girl.

'The school was very supportive, but because she moved up to secondary school with her peer group, everybody knew.

'In the first week, she was called a "tranny" and a "man-beast". She was spat on and attacked in the corridors. Within her first six months of being at that school, she took four overdoses.

'We then pulled her out of school, but after a few months she decided to go back.

'Each year, the bullying and isolation got worse, and Nicki started harming herself. At the beginning of year nine, I transferred her to another secondary school, but unfortunately the kids there found out.

'At that point, I withdrew her from school completely, and the education welfare office found her a place at a Specialist Inclusive Learning Centre, which is a unit for children who can't cope with mainstream schooling for various health reasons.'

'My trans daughter'

Going through puberty

'When Nicki started puberty, I wanted her to get the type of treatment that's offered in the Netherlands, where puberty is blocked before major physical changes take place.

'I felt that if she was going to change her mind about being a girl, she would have done so by now.

'The Tavistock Clinic wouldn't give her hormone blockers. [The Tavistock and Portman follows British guidelines, which at the time suggested not introducing hormone blockers until the latter stages of puberty. Since January 2011, the age at which hormonal treatment may be offered has been lowered from 16 to 12, under a research study that is being carried out by the Tavistock and Portman into the effects of hormone blockers earlier in puberty.]

'In the end, we went to a doctor in the US. I found him through the WPATH network (The World Professional Association for Transgender Health). Nicki was 13 when she started taking hormone blockers. It's put her male puberty on hold, and given her time to think.

'If she hadn't been given blockers, she would have suffered the psychological agony of going through male puberty. She told me she would have killed herself. Nowadays, you'd never guess that she was born male.

'If at any point Nicki told me that she wasn't sure that this was the right thing for her, we'd simply stop the injections and male puberty would go ahead.

'For Nicki, the next step is starting hormones and surgery as soon as she can.

'During the first few years of secondary school, I was constantly in fear for Nicki's life. It was so distressing to watch her go through all of this.

'Now it's a million times better. She's a typical teenage girl, and it's a blessing. She leaves a mess, she borrows my clothes, my make-up and my perfume. I never thought she'd reach this stage. She still has to face many more hurdles but she's looking forward to adulthood.'

**The names in this article have been changed*

Where to get help

Sharon, who tells her story here, says that the most helpful thing was speaking to other families who've been through the same thing. The charity Mermaids provides family support for children and teenagers with gender identity issues, and it can put you in touch with other parents with similar experiences.

Further information

The story above reflects one mother's experience. Because gender identity issues are complex and each case is different, Sharon's story shouldn't be seen as typical.

For more information on gender identity issues in children and young people, see the *Teenagers and gender identity* and *Worried about a child with gender identity issues?* pages on the NHS Choices website (www.nhs.uk).

Last reviewed 27 May 2011

www.nhs.uk

Activities

Brainstorm

Brainstorm to find out what you know about sexual orientation and gender identity.

1. What does LGBT stand for?

....

....

....

2. What are the differences between heterosexual, homosexual and bisexual? What does transgender mean?

....

....

....

Oral activities

3. Plan an informative class talk about being transgender to help educate people. Be sure to give the definition of key words associated with transgender people.

NOTES..........

....

....

4. Get into pairs and role play the following situation: imagine that one of you is the parent and the other is the child who thinks they might be gay and have decided to 'come out'.

NOTES..........

....

....

Moral dilemma

5. 'Being gay is just a phase young people go through.' Discuss this with a partner.

Activities

Research activities

6. Research a charity that helps support young people struggling with their sexual orientation/identity. Write some notes on your findings.

CONCLUSIONS..

....

....

7. Research famous and notable LGBT people who have contributed to and made an impact on society. This can include artists/scientists/writers/musicians and composers and so on. For example, actor and comedian Stephen Fry, Jane Lynch who plays the aggressive cheerleading coach Sue Sylvester in the TV show Glee or Jane Addams, the first American woman to be awarded the Nobel Peace Prize in 1931.

NOTES..

....

....

Written activities

Complete the following activities in your exercise books or on a sheet of paper.

8. Your friend confides in you that they think they might be gay. They are worried and scared that people will bully them for being homosexual. Write them a supportive letter about where they can turn to for help and advice.

9. Think about a time when you felt someone treated you differently because of something that you really liked and started to call you nasty names. How did this make you feel? Write a diary entry concentrating on your feelings when this happened.

Design activities

10. Design an informative pamphlet about transgender terminology for your local youth club. Choose a couple definitions from *Trans terminology* on pages 10 and 11 and explain what they mean.

11. Select a key moment from the *LGB & T timeline* on pages 12 and 13 and draw a cartoon about it.

My homophobic bullying story

Doug Faulkner is a comedy writer and performer. He was bullied throughout secondary school.

Because of his experience, he's passionate about tackling homophobic bullying in schools. He describes what happened to him.

How did the bullying start?

'I've always been an extrovert, and I was quite effeminate when I started secondary school. At the time, I considered it part of my personality and nothing to do with sex or sexuality. It was just who I was.

'Because I was very confident, the older kids wanted to put me down, and people in my own year group joined in.

'It started with homophobic name calling. The first time I heard the word "gay" was in a hateful context, and I didn't even know what it meant. I just thought I was uncool.

'By the time I was in the third year, I was being bullied a lot. It was always homophobic bullying. It would happen on the way to school on the bus, between lessons, sometimes during lessons and on the bus home. It wasn't just verbal abuse but physical abuse too. Once, on the way home, my hair was set on fire.

'It took a lot of strength to get out of the house and face the bullying. Being ridiculed was part of my daily life.

'I was at the bottom of all my classes. My self-esteem was so low that I was almost suicidal. I didn't know who or where I was. All I knew was that nearly everyone had decided that I was loathsome, vile and unnatural.'

'After about a year of counselling, I started to get a bit more confident.'

Did the school do anything?

'I'm dyslexic, so my school made me do an IQ test in the third year. I had the highest IQ in my year, but I wasn't doing well academically because my self-confidence was so low. So the school sent me for counselling when I was 14.

'After counselling, my mum said to me: "Do you think it upsets you so much when people call you names because you think what they're saying might be true?"

'I said to Mum, "I'm 14. That's not a decision I'm prepared to make now. I have the right to experiment and find out about myself. But I'm not being given that right at school. They're telling me what I am, and that it's disgusting."

'The counselling helped because it gave me a chance to express myself. After about a year or so of counselling, I became more confident. I'd find different ways to try to stop the bullying, such as being the class clown or being nice to the right people.'

Recorded hate crime from regional forces in England, Wales and Northern Ireland during the calendar year 2010 (all in trans and sexual orientation categories).

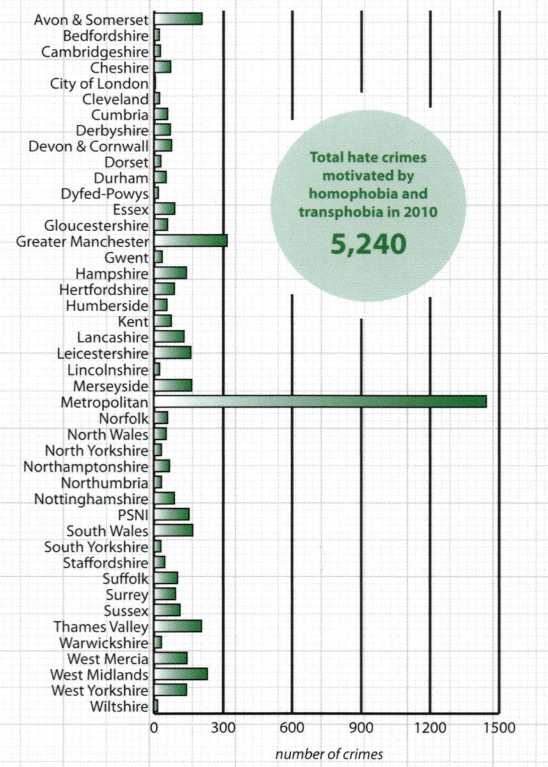

Source: Association of Chief Police Officers (ACPO) © ACPO 2011

My homophobic bullying story

How did the bullying make you feel?

'I'd get a sinking feeling. As soon as I walked along a corridor I knew it was going to happen. It happened a lot in certain areas, such as walking from class to class or going to and from school.

'It gave me a victim mentality. I either loathed myself or I loathed everybody else for making me feel like this.

'Leaving school after GCSEs was the only way out. During the five years after I left school, the culture towards homosexuality changed. I came out properly to my friends when I was 19, and to my family when I was 20.'

Has your experience at school affected you in later life?

'On the negative side, I find it very difficult to have long-term relationships because it's difficult to trust people. I'm scared they're going to turn around and be hurtful.

'On the positive side, it's helped me understand how different we all are, and how that difference makes us stronger.

'Everyone deserves to feel positive and unique, and happy with that uniqueness.

'I also respect people's need to have space to discover who they are, because I didn't have much space.'

Where to find help

Schools have a legal duty to ensure that homophobic bullying is dealt with.

For further information and advice about homophobic bullying, look at these three websites:

EACH

EACH is a charity for young people and adults affected by homophobia and transphobia. It has a telephone helpline for young people who are experiencing homophobic or transphobic bullying. You can call Actionline on 0808 1000 143 on weekdays, 9am-4.30pm. Calls are free from landlines and most mobiles.

Stonewall: Education for All

Stonewall is a charity that campaigns for equal rights for lesbians, gay men and bisexual people. Their Education for All campaign tackles homophobia and homophobic bullying in schools across the UK. On the Education for All website, you can find case studies, facts and figures about homophobic bullying in schools and advice for young people and teachers.

Schools Out

Schools Out is an organisation that works towards equality in education for lesbian, gay, bisexual and trans people. Find out more about your rights at school in the Student Toolkit section of the site.

2 June 2011

www.nhs.uk

Homophobic crime

If you are a victim of crime and think that you were targeted because of your sexuality, or the sexuality of someone you know, find out about how the police will help you when you report it.

What is homophobic crime?

If someone becomes a victim of crime because of their sexuality, then this is classed as a crime where homophobia is one of the main motivations.

Homophobic hate crime can happen anywhere and is often based on prejudice and stereotypes. Any homophobic crime will be taken very seriously by the police. Sentences for crimes proven to have a homophobic motive behind them will be tougher and the reporting of homophobic crimes will be treated as seriously as racial hate crimes.

Types of homophobic crime

Homophobic crime can affect victims in many ways. For example, someone could be assaulted or robbed because their attacker does not like people who they see as different to them.

Other victims may have homophobic graffiti and slogans painted on their house or belongings by people who suspect that someone who lives there is gay.

Reporting a homophobic crime

If you have been a victim of a crime, or witnessed a crime taking place, and you think that there may have been a homophobic motive behind it, you should mention this to the police when you are giving your statement.

Victims of homophobic crime may be reluctant to report the incident to the police because they are not comfortable talking about their sexuality to people they do not know. They may feel that they will not be listened to or taken seriously.

Most local police forces have a special unit that is dedicated to dealing with incidents of homophobic crime. Officers who work in these units have had special training on how to deal with issues of homophobia. If you would feel more comfortable talking to someone like this, ask to speak to them when you contact the police station.

Homophobic bullying

If you are still at school, you may be bullied because others think you are gay. Although this is not a crime that you can report to the police, being bullied is still an upsetting experience and you shouldn't put up with it.

Bullying doesn't just happen at school. You may be being harassed, victimised or picked on at work because your colleagues think you're gay.

Whether you are at school or work, you should let a teacher or a manager know if you're being bullied so that they can do something about it.

www.direct.gov.uk

More gay couples tie the knot

Almost ten times more gay and lesbian couples have formed civil partnerships than was originally predicted when the law was introduced.

Tim Ross, Political Correspondent

Last year 6,795 couples formalised their relationships in civil partnership ceremonies in the UK, an increase of 6.4% since 2010, according to official figures.

The number of dissolutions rose by more than a quarter, but statisticians said this simply reflected the increasing number of people in civil partnerships.

The figures, from the Office for National Statistics, will fuel debate about David Cameron's plans to grant full marriage rights to same-sex couples.

Since 2005, gay and lesbian couples have been able officially to register their relationships as civil partnerships, giving them effectively the same legal rights as married couples, but they cannot call themselves 'married'.

The Coalition has changed the law to enable churches and other religious groups to host civil partnership ceremonies for the first time.

More gay couples tie the knot

The Prime Minister and his Liberal Democrat deputy, Nick Clegg, want to go further and allow same-sex couples to marry.

Their plan, which is currently undergoing a public consultation, has provoked fierce criticism from religious leaders, including the Anglican Archbishop of York, and the Roman Catholic Archbishop of Westminster.

Scores of back-bench Conservative MPs and a number of government ministers also oppose the planned new gay marriage law, arguing that it is a 'distraction' from the Coalition's core task of reviving the economy.

The ONS figures showed that the number of people forming civil partnerships had far exceeded original expectations.

In 2004, before the reform was introduced, the then Labour government estimated that between 11,000 and 22,000 people would be likely to take-up civil partnerships in Great Britain by 2010.

However, by the end of last year, the total had reached 106,834, which the ONS noted was 'much higher' than officials had originally forecast.

The figures also showed that lesbian couples were more likely than gay couples to dissolve their partnerships.

By the end of 2011, 2.2 per cent of gay civil partnerships in the UK had ended in dissolution, compared to 4.6 per cent of lesbian partnerships.

Overall, there were 672 dissolutions in 2011, up from 522 in 2010. However, as the number of people entering civil partnerships continues to rise, the number of couples separating is also expected to increase.

Male couples on average formed civil partnerships at the age of just over 40, while lesbian women were typically 38 years old.

There were significant decreases in the numbers of same-sex couples forming civil partnerships in Wales and Northern Ireland. Stonewall, the gay rights organisation, suggested this could indicate that people were waiting for the law to change to allow them to marry instead.

Under the Government's plans, only civil marriage would be changed to allow same sex couples to wed. Religious marriage would be unaffected.

A Home Office spokesman said: 'This Government believes society is stronger when couples commit to each other, which is why it is so encouraging to see more same-sex couples entering civil partnerships.

'We now want to make it possible for all couples, regardless of their gender, to get married in a civil ceremony.

'Under our proposals couples who are already in a civil partnership will be able to convert it into a marriage if they wish to. We will announce the results of our consultation by the end of the year.'

31 July 2012

Mini glossary

Dissolution *– similar to a divorce, dissolution refers to the legal undoing of a union, such as a civil partnership*

www.telegraph.co.uk

Social exclusion and sexual orientation

Information from Stonewall.

Overview

People tend to think that the majority of the 'gay community' is white, male and middle-class, with high levels of disposable income. However, this does not accurately reflect the different backgrounds of gay people in Britain.

Lesbian, gay and bisexual people are just as likely to be from low-income backgrounds as from anywhere else. Gay people from more well-off backgrounds are simply more visible than those from other backgrounds.

It is also well documented that discrimination can lead to social exclusion. Therefore gay people are in fact likely to experience greater economic disadvantages and social exclusion in some circumstances just because of their sexual orientation.

What we know

No-one knows how many gay people there are in Britain. Due to the fear of discrimination, it is likely that many studies tend to underestimate numbers. However, the government estimates that six per cent of the population, around 3.6 million people, are lesbian, gay or bisexual.

Stonewall's position is that if six per cent of the population are gay, then six per cent of those from less-well-off backgrounds are likely to be gay. We also know from our research that gay people face a wide range of challenges and discrimination that can add to social exclusion.

Stonewall's survey of 1,658 lesbian, gay and bisexual people, Serves You Right, found that gay people expect poorer treatment from public services including social housing, criminal justice and health services.

Serves You Right also found that nearly one in five gay people say they have experienced bullying from their colleagues because of their sexual orientation. Discrimination in the workplace can lead to people leaving their jobs and becoming unemployed. Lesbian, gay and bisexual people in working-class groups are 50 per cent more likely to experience work-place bullying than those in middle-class groups.

Stonewall's survey of 1,140 young lesbian, gay and bisexual people, The School Report, found that 65 per cent of young people had experienced homophobic bullying. Seven in ten feel this has an impact on their work, and half have skipped school at some point because of it. Stonewall's The Gay British Crime Survey found one in five lesbian, gay and bisexual people have experienced a homophobic hate crime in the last three years.

Research shows that discrimination can cause mental health problems, including anxiety and depression.

Stonewall's report on a survey of 6,000 lesbian and bisexual women, Prescription for Change, found that half of young women under the age of 20 have self-harmed in the last year. Research indicates that young lesbian, gay and bisexual

Social exclusion and sexual orientation

people are more likely to be at risk of homelessness because of bullying at school and rejection from the family home.

Generally, discrimination impacts on health and well-being, and this can affect social inclusion.

Stonewall often hears from lesbian, gay and bisexual people who are experiencing difficulties accessing the correct benefits via our freephone information service. This is often because local authorities and benefits offices get confused about the rights of same-sex couples. Many organisations are still not clear on the rights and responsibilities of lesbian, gay and bisexual people, which can lead to heightened economic exclusion.

Information from Stonewall. © 2012 Stonewall

www.stonewall.org.uk

What we have done

From 2009, government research has started to include questions relating to sexual orientation. Stonewall lobbied for this change and welcome it. In future, this will mean more accurate data will be available on the social exclusion faced by lesbian, gay and bisexual people.

However, as questions relating to sexual orientation are relatively new, it is anticipated that it will take several years to secure completely accurate data.

What we are currently doing

Stonewall continue to work with government and respond to consultations on social exclusion and deprivation where relevant to lesbian, gay and bisexual people.

For example, we engage with the independent National Equality Panel tasked with investigating the relationships between different aspects of inequality in people's economic situations, and their other characteristics and circumstances.

There are complex interactions both between multiple equality strands and also wider conditions of economic and social disadvantage. We recognise that more in-depth research into the social exclusion and economic disadvantage experienced by lesbian, gay and bisexual people is needed and we continue to work to develop appropriate research methods in this challenging area.

If you require more information on Stonewall's work in social exclusion please contact 08000 50 20 20 or info@stonewall.org.uk

Mini glossary

Disposable income – *after paying their taxes, the money a person has left from their income*

Social exclusion – *when rights and opportunities are taken away from people just because they belong to a certain community*

Factbox: lesbian, gay, bisexual and transgender rights around the world

May 17 is International Day against homo- and transphobia. Here is a snapshot of the state of legal rights of lesbian, gay, bisexual and transgender people globally.

By Astrid Zweynert

- Homosexuality is illegal in 76 countries, including five that have the death penalty (Mauritania, Sudan as well as 12 northern states in Nigeria and the southern parts of Somalia, Iran, Saudi Arabia, Yemen).
- Motive for hatred based on sexual orientation is prohibited in just 24 countries.
- Africa has gone from bad to worse in the past ten years, with 36 countries now having laws criminalising homosexuality. They are: Algeria, Angola, Botswana, Burundi, Cameroon (1972), Comoros, Egypt, Eritrea, Ethiopia, Gambia, Ghana, Guinea, Kenya, Lesotho, Liberia, Libya, Malawi, Mauritania, Mauritius, Morocco, Mozambique, Namibia, Nigeria, São Tomé and Principe, Senegal, Seychelles, Sierra Leone, Somalia, Sudan, Swaziland, Tanzania, Togo, Tunisia, Uganda, Zambia, Zimbabwe.

Since 2005 same-sex couples have been able to enter into civil partnerships. While civil partnerships offer the same legal rights as marriage, same-sex couples are not able to marry. Which of the following best reflects your view?

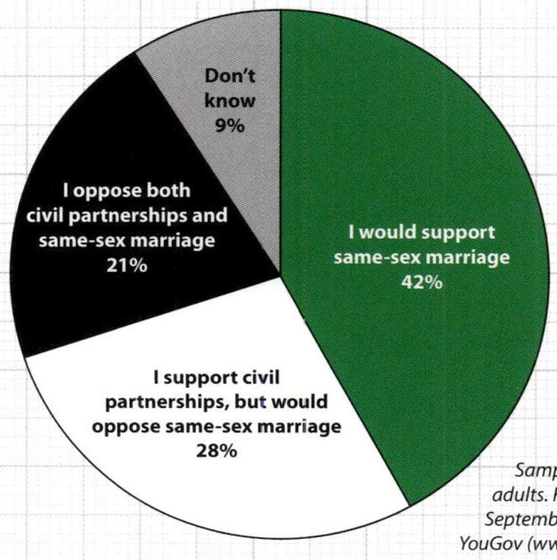

Sample size: 2601 GB adults. Fieldwork: 20-21 September 2011. Source: YouGov (www.yougov.com)

- More than half of Asian and Middle Eastern countries still criminalise homosexuality but there have been some notable steps in India, where gay sex was decriminalised in 2009, and Nepal and Pakistan recognising the third gender. Homosexuality is illegal in Afghanistan, Bangladesh, Bhutan, Brunei, some parts of Indonesia (South Sumatra and Aceh Province), Iran, Kuwait, Lebanon, Malaysia, Maldives, Myanmar, Oman, Pakistan, Qatar, Saudi Arabia, Singapore, Sri Lanka, Syria, Turkish Republic of Northern Cyprus (internationally unrecognised), Turkmenistan, United Arab Emirates, Uzbekistan, Yemen, as well as the Palestinian Territories.
- In Latin America and the Caribbean homosexuality is illegal in Antigua and Barbuda, Barbados, Belize, Dominica, Grenada, Guyana, Jamaica, St Kitts and Nevis, St Lucia, St Vincent and the Grenadines, Trinidad and Tobago.
- None of the European countries can claim to provide full legal equality for lesbian, gay, bisexual and transgender people but Cyprus, Italy, Latvia, Malta, Turkey and Ukraine are the countries ranking the lowest in terms of legal equality.

Source: The International Lesbian, Gay, Bisexual, Trans and Intersex Association, 2011

Activities

Brainstorm

Brainstorm to find out what you know about LGBT Rights.

1. What is a homophobic crime?

....

....

....

2. Is homosexuality accepted all around the world? If not, where?

....

....

....

Oral activity

3. Unchallenged homophobic language is so ingrained in everyday language that even the word 'gay' has come to mean anything worthless or without value. Talk about words which form part of a homophobic bully's vocabulary. What images do they bring to mind? Why are they so harmful?

NOTES..

....

....

....

....

Moral dilemmas

4. You find out that a boy at your school is bisexual. Now your group of friends have started to shun him and exclude him from social events. Is this right? What do you do?
5. 'Homosexuality is illegal in 76 countries, including five that have the death penalty.' Should homosexuality be illegal? Discuss this statement as a class.

Activities

Research activities

6. Are schools doing enough to educate students about LGBT and LGBT rights? Using the Internet, magazines and newspapers, research different programmes and schemes that have been introduced into schools to raise awareness.

CONCLUSIONS..

....

....

7. Find out about 'LGBT Pride' or 'Gay Pride Day'. Come up with some ideas for a similar day for your local neighbourhood and community. Think about when the day should be held and what the celebrations would consist of. Do you think having a 'LGBT Day' is a good idea?

NOTES..

....

....

Written activities

Complete the following activities in your exercise books or on a sheet of paper.

8. Make a list of all the different forms of homophobic discrimination you can think of. Why do you think these take place? What should be done about it?

9. Read *More gay couples tie the knot on* pages 21 and 22. Write a brief summary of the article.

Design activities

10. Many organisations are still not clear on the rights and responsibilities of lesbian, gay and bisexual people. Read *Social exclusion and sexual orientation* on pages 23 and 24. Create a leaflet for organisations to inform them about LGBT rights and the rights of same-sex couples.

11. Schools have a legal duty to ensure that homophobic bullying is dealt with. Design a poster to be displayed in your school about tackling homophobic bullying.

Key facts

- 'Homosexuality is not a mental disorder and the APA [American Psychological Association] opposes all portrayals of lesbian, gay and bisexual people as mentally ill and in need of treatment due to their sexual orientation.' (page 2)
- LGBT people come from all walks of life, are black, brown, white and all shades in between, may or may not be disabled. Some children may look or dress differently to their peers but this does not mean that they identify as LGBT, or that they will when they are older. (page 6)
- In 2004 it was estimated that there were 124,672 same-gender-attracted pupils in British secondary schools. This is approximately 100 pupils in a school of 2,000. (page 7)
- Gender variance may be detected in children as young as two, and a high proportion of people who have gender reassignment as adults say that they knew that they were trans while in primary school, even if they lacked the language to express this. (page 7)
- It is estimated that one in ten adults identify as lesbian, gay or bisexual. (page 7)
- Lesbians, gay men and bisexuals comprise around 6% of the population, or 3.5 million people, according to government estimates. (page 9)
- A third of gay staff hide their sexual orientation from their employers and co-workers, yet 'out' employees in safe environments earn 50% more than their closeted peers. (page 9)
- Clinical protocols recommend that a transsexual person transitioning must live for one year in their 'new' gender, full-time and uninterrupted, before being referred for GAS [Gender Affirmation Surgery]. In England, the NHS adopted a two-year system: elsewhere it is one year. (page 11)
- In 1993, the Government removed homosexuality from its list of psychiatric disorders in England and Wales (Scottish government removed it in 2000). (page 13)
- In 2000, the age of consent for homosexual sex equalised with heterosexual sex, set at 16 for the UK and 17 for Northern Ireland. (page 13)
- Stonewall's survey of 1,140 young lesbian, gay and bisexual people, The School Report, found that 65 per cent of young people had experienced homophobic bullying. Seven in ten feel this has an impact on their work, and half have skipped school at some point because of it. (page 23)
- Homosexuality is illegal in 76 countries, including five that have the death penalty (Mauritania, Sudan as well as 12 northern states in Nigeria and the southern parts of Somalia, Iran, Saudi Arabia, Yemen). (page 25)

Glossary

Asexual – *A person who does not have a sexual orientation and is not sexually attracted to anyone.*

Bisexual – *A person who is emotionally and physically attracted to both men and women. The person may feel a stronger attraction to one sex over another, or feel attraction to different sexes at different points in their lives.*

Coming out – *'Coming out' happens when an LGBT person feels ready to tell their family and friends about their sexual identity. Coming out is a big step, especially as people fear negative reactions to their announcement. Therefore it is not unusual for someone to not be 'fully out' and only tell a select few people.*

Gender reassignment – *Also known as sex reassignment surgery, this involves changing a person's physical appearance to become their desired gender of choice. This includes altering their external gender organs and hormonal balances.*

Heterosexual – *Someone who identifies themselves as heterosexual is attracted to people of the opposite sex to themselves. It is often referred to as being 'straight'.*

Homophobia – *The fear or hatred of people who are attracted to the same sex as themselves (e.g. disliking lesbians, gay men and bisexuals).*

Homosexual – *A person who is attracted to members of the same sex as themselves. Men who like men are known as gay. Women who like women are known as lesbians. Homosexuality used to be illegal and viewed as a mental illness, but this is no longer the case and is now becoming more widely accepted.*

LGBT – *LGBT stands for Lesbian, Gay, Bisexual and Transgender. It is shorthand for referring to sexual identities other than heterosexual.*

Sexual identity – *How a person identifies themselves physically, whether it be male, female, in between or neither.*

Sexual orientation – *A person's sexual identity; defining a person's attraction either towards members of the same sex (homosexual), the opposite sex (heterosexual) or both (bisexual).*

Transgender or 'trans' – *A person who lives and identifies themselves as a member of the opposite gender, different to the gender they were assigned at birth. They chose to live their life as what they feel is their correct and real gender. They may or may not chose to undergo surgery to physically look like their gender of choice.*

Transphobia – *The fear or hatred of people who are transgender or transsexual.*